DEDICATION

I dedicate this book to my two beautiful children and my loving wife who have been nothing short of being my light and joy throughout the years.

Copyright 2017 by Jonathan S. Walker - All rights reserved.

The following eBook is reproduced below with the goal of providing information that is as accurate and reliable as possible. Regardless, purchasing this eBook can be seen as consent to the fact that both the publisher and the author of this book are in no way experts on the topics discussed within and that any recommendations or suggestions that are made herein are for entertainment purposes only. Professionals should be consulted as needed prior to undertaking any of the action endorsed herein.

This declaration is deemed fair and valid by both the American Bar Association and the Committee of Publishers Association and is legally binding throughout the United States.

Recruiting & Retailing Mastery For Network Marketing

How You Can Become the Next Network Marketing

JONATHAN S. WALKER

Copyright © 2017 Jonathan S. Walker

All rights reserved.

Furthermore, the transmission, duplication or reproduction of any of the following work including specific information will be considered an illegal act irrespective of if it is done electronically or in print. This extends to creating a secondary or tertiary copy of the work or a recorded copy and is only allowed with express written consent from the Publisher. All additional right reserved.

The information in the following pages is broadly considered to be a truthful and accurate account of facts and as such any inattention, use or misuse of the information in question by the reader will render any resulting actions solely under their purview. There are no scenarios in which the publisher or the original author of this work can be in any fashion deemed liable for any hardship or damages that may befall them after undertaking information described herein.

Additionally, the information in the following pages is intended only for informational purposes and should thus be thought of as universal. As befitting its nature, it is presented without assurance regarding its prolonged validity or interim quality. Trademarks that are mentioned are done without written consent and can in no way be considered an endorsement from the trademark holder.

VIP Subscriber List

Dear Reader, If you would like to receive latest tips and tricks on internet marketing, exclusive strategies, upcoming books & promotions, and more, do subscribe to my mailing list in the link below! I will be giving away a free book that you can download right away as well after you subscribe to show my appreciation!

Here's the link: http://bit.do/jonathanswalker

CONTENTS

Part 1

Introduction

Chapter 1: Understanding Network Marketing

Chapter 2: Tips on How To Find Network Marketing Success

Chapter 3: Successful Network Marketing Strategies & How To Find Your Audience

Chapter 4: Common Mistakes The New Network Marketers Make & How To Avoid Them

Part 2

Chapter 1: Who Are You Talking To?

Chapter 2: What Are Your Motivations

Chapter 3: How Will You Prepare?

Chapter 4: Which Tactics Are Indispensable?

Chapter 5: The Supreme Tactic – Follow-Up Communication

Part 3

Chapter 1: Prospecting – What Is It?

Chapter 2: Techniques To Use For Prospecting

Chapter 3: How To BE Prospecting In Your Prospecting

Chapter 4: Prospecting Myths

Chapter 5: Tools To Use For Prospecting

Chapter 6: Tips For Prospecting

Introduction

Congratulations on purchasing your personal copy of *Recruiting & Retailing Mastery for Network Marketing: How You Can Become the Next Network Marketing Superstar in Your Company*. Thank you for doing so.

The following chapters will discuss everything that you need to know in order to become the best network marketing employee within your respective company. This book will go beyond simply discussing what network marketing is and how you can get started in a great career. It will also discuss how you can take your passion for network marketing and create a guaranteed path of success for yourself. Once you understand the tactics that are presented in this book, you will have the tools that you need to excel within your company through a concrete set of goals and steps that you can take to improve yourself. No one wants to be considered mediocre, and after reading this book you will have the tools that you need to truly become reputable and successful.

You will discover what network marketing is and some great tips on getting started in this type of professional environment. We will also look at how you can create a schedule for yourself that will lead to more concrete and lasting results. Another topic that this book will discuss is the idea of how to narrow your target market, so that you're not advertising and spending precious time on people who are not truly interested in purchasing the product that you're selling.

The last chapter will document common mistakes that beginner network marketing professionals make. By discussing and being aware of these common mistakes, the hope is that you will be less likely to make these same mistakes in the future. Specific topics within this chapter will include how not to generate leads, how to properly interact with the people who are working underneath of you, and how to present your product in the best way possible.

There are plenty of books on this subject on the market, thanks again for choosing this one! Every effort was made to ensure it is full of as much useful information as possible. Please enjoy!

Congratulations on purchasing your personal copy of *Recruiting & Retailing Mastery for Network Marketing: How You Can Become the Next Network Marketing Superstar in Your Company.* Enjoy the remainder of this book.

Chapter 1: Understanding Network Marketing

Before we get into how you can optimize a career for yourself in network marketing, we must first begin by fully understanding what network marketing is all about. Specifically, this chapter is going to focus on the topics of lead generation, recruiting and how to train the recruits that you eventually choose. It will also discuss the different types of network marketing hierarchies that exist, so that you will be able to figure out the type of structure that a company works within once you begin to look for network marketing work. All of these topics are essential when seeking to understand how network marketing functions, and without being informed about these topics the rest of the book will make less sense.

What is Network Marketing?

Network marketing is also known as multi-level marketing. This type of marketing can be best defined as a type of marketing strategy that is multi-tiered and often hierarchal in nature. Typically, a larger company or corporation will incentivize individuals to sell products on the company's behalf. In exchange for the salesman or saleswoman's time, the company will provide them with a commissioned percentage of their total sales. In other words, the corporation will provide the individual with the product to sell, and the individual will then be responsible for selling the products. Some examples of popular network marketing companies that you may have heard of include Mary Kay, Omnilife, and Rodan and Fields.

How Does It Work?

A network marketing business should not be too difficult to understand. If you come across one that is difficult to understand, you should be weary because there is a chance that it could be a front for some type of scam. Typically, once you decide on the company for whom you want to work, you will be required to pay a small fee. This fee will usually not be more than a few hundred dollars. In exchange for your money, the company in question will provide you with a sample set of products that you can then sell to family, friends, or clients. If you decide to stick with the network marketing company after this trial period, you will still be paying the company so that you can sell the products that they're giving you, but the hope of any network marketing salesperson is to sell enough product to cover the cost of the product itself and also make a profit.

Often, an additional incentive that a network marketing company will put on an individual salesperson is the incentive to recruit other members who can work underneath of (you), the original salesperson. When you recruit more people to work underneath of you, you're provided with additional payment from the company who owns the rights to the product, and you're also paid when these salespeople make money as well. As you can see, this structure is hierarchal, with the product company being at the top and the people who are working underneath people like you at the bottom. You may start as a person who is low on the hierarchy, but the goal for a serious network marketer is to eventually become the middle manager who is recruiting people to work sales.

The Three Elements of Network Marketing

Typically, once you are involved with a network marketing company, there are going to be three elements of the business of which you should be aware. These elements include the notions of lead generation, recruiting methods, and adequately training your new recruits. Let's look at each of these elements separately:

Lead Generation: Lead generation is an essential aspect of any successful network marketer. If you don't start your network marketing career with a lot of leads, then it will be less likely that you will make a lot of sales. A great tactic to use when you're first starting out is to turn to the internet. Establishing a good online presence as a network marketer will be the subject of a subsequent chapter.

Recruiting Methods: Good recruiting methods are also important for any aspiring network marketer.

While you may be the low man (or woman) on the totem pole when you're first starting out in a reputable network marketing company, you're only going to start making real money once you are recruiting your own sales people who can generate commissions on their sales for you. A great way to recruit people for sales is to talk to people who are interested in selling about the *results* of your own sales and the perks of working for the company.

Recruit Training: Once you have found people who are interested in working under you, you have to know how to train them properly. Otherwise, you will be managing people for free because they will not be making any money for you! An important aspect of training involves you taking on the role of mentor or coach for these new salespeople. You are going to want these people to feel as if they can rely on you for support when they need it, along with encouragement along the way. Without this support on your end and the ability to provide these people with strong direction, these people will be more likely to find work elsewhere.

Single-Level Versus Multi-Level Marketing

Lastly, it's important to understand how multi-level marketing differs from single-level marketing. It's safe to say that if you're looking to be as profitable as possible, you are going to gravitate towards multi-level marketing. With single-level marketing, you are still going to purchase product from a larger company, but you are not going to have anyone working underneath of you. This is the key difference between single-level marketing and multi-level marketing. As an aspiring network marketer, you may start out as single-level, but your ultimate goal (if you're serious), is to work towards being a multi-level marketer with employees who you manage, motivate, and from whom you receive a commissioned profit.

Chapter 2: Tips on How to Find Network Marketing Success

Now that you have an understanding of what network marketing is and the basic concepts guiding this professional niche, it's time to look at some key tips that will help you get started on a successful path as quickly as possible. Without understanding and implementing the tips that are presented in this chapter, your initial sales are likely to be lower than they should be, and this will deter you from continuing with this potentially lucrative business. Additionally, these tips will help you to feel more confident as you move forward in your pursuit of becoming a successful network marketing agent.

Tip 1: Choose the Company You Want to Work for Carefully

It's likely that you've heard about how pyramid schemes can be disguised as legitimate network marketing businesses. Without getting into the details of a pyramid scheme, they are a way to deceitfully take people's money and you definitely do not want to become part of one. This is why it's extremely important that you choose a network marketing company to work for that you know is reputable and will be able to provide you with lucrative results. Here are some great things to research about the company, prior to committing yourself to it:

1. Has the company been around for at least five years? Most network marketing firms fail within two years of being open. If you can find one that's been in business for at least five years, it's a sign that you may have found a good one.

2. Is the company well-funded? A good piece of advice is to look to work for a company that is publicly traded on the stock market, because this means that they are required to publicly disclose how much money they're worth. You want to make sure that you're working for a company that can pay your commissions and provide you with great incentives (like the notorious Mary Kay pink Cadillac!).

3. Does the company offer a unique service or product? You don't want to be trying to sell something that no one feels like they need in their lives. Before committing to a company, it'd be a good idea to make sure that this same type of product is not available somewhere else for a discount, and that there is not a ton of competition within the market for this particular product.

Tip 2: Analyze the Mentorship within the Program

In any type of network marketing program, the more experienced leaders within the program should be willing to help any newbie out via mentoring for at least thirty days. You want to make sure that this type of mentoring is in fact occurring within the network marketing company in which you choose to partake. Otherwise, it's likely that you will end up feeling lost, insecure, and unsuccessful. Within the industry, when a new member of group is not care for, it's known as "orphaning". Don't let yourself be an orphan. Do adequate research of the company prior to committing to it, so that there is no way that this can happen to you.

Tip 3: Hire an Accountant

Even though you are going to technically be working for a large company, you will still be responsible for taking care of your own taxes and other types of financial filings. Remember, you are going to get paid on commission most likely, and this means that you may have to provide invoices to the company that document the sales that you've made. Especially within the first year of being in business, you're going to want to make sure that you're doing everything right from the perspective of the government. Unless you have a background in accounting, you should do yourself a favor and hire someone who can assist you in these types of matters. These days, you may not even have to hire someone, and can instead look into accounting software for yourself.

Tip 4: Be Hesitant to Quit Your Day Job

Even though it's likely that you're interested in network marketing because it will provide you with flexible working hours, this does not mean that you should eagerly quit your full-time job as soon as you start working for the network marketing company. These networks take time to grow and take hold, and you don't want to be desolate as you work towards developing income in this new and exciting field. Once you start to make more money, you'll be given a better idea of how much you can expect to make through these means. It's only when you're confident that you can make a living wage that you should quit your current job to pursue network marketing to the fullest extent possible; unless of course, you have a spouse or someone else who has agreed to support you during this period of time.

Chapter 3: Successful Network Marketing Strategies and How to Find Your Audience

Now that we've gone over some tips that you should be thinking about when you're first getting started in network marketing, we are now going to turn our attention to the next step in this progression towards overall network marketing success. This chapter is going to be focusing on some of the key tactics that you can implement once you've chosen a company and are ready to really start going after clients to make money. Being in the network marketing business means that you're essentially a highly visible salesperson. This being the case, you want to make sure that your sales platforms are all planned carefully, smartly, and in a way that will yield real results.

Planning Your Approach

While the internet is certainly going to help your

sales outreach, you're also going to want to take some time to truly figure out how much money you plan on making and how you can reach this point. One of the first questions that you should be able to succinctly answer prior to making a single sale is what type of business do you want this to be? Are you looking to make network marketing only a gig for yourself, or are you looking to recruit others and eventually make a small piece of an empire your own? It's generally recommended that if you're looking to make network marketing a part-time gig, you should be willing to devote between 3 to 10 hours of your time per week to the business. On the other hand, if know that you want to recruit people and eventually manage a small network yourself, expect to devote at least 15 hours a week to this venture. Knowing this information up front will help you to plan your weeks accordingly.

Additionally, you're going to want to take advantage of any training that the product's company can provide you. Most network marketing companies, if they're legitimate, will typically offer trainings and seminars to their salespeople. These meetings can take place over the internet or in person, and you should try to attend as many as you can. Not only will this help you financially if these trainings are paid, but they will also allow you to potentially meet mentors within the group and network with other people who are in your same position as a beginner. Networking is an extremely important aspect of this type of marketing structure. As you work through planning your approach, a good piece of advice to keep in mind is that you can never spend too much time attending promotional and informational events that are related to the product that you're selling.

Your Online Presence

These days, the internet is a powerful tool that any business should be using. This fact is no different for someone who is interested in network marketing. Let's take a look at some of the ways that you can easily gain exposure via an online platform.

Contact Reputable Blogs

You may or may not be aware of the fact that successful bloggers are also people who are constantly trying to make money through their writing. A primary way that a blogger is able to make money is through advertising. Wouldn't it be fabulous if a blogger could advertise your product for you to their own audience? Of course, the blogger will charge you a small fee in exchange for this service, but the upside to this fact is that you can arrange to only pay the blogger when a sale is made through their website. Some bloggers will want to review your product on their site and hope that this generates some interest, while others will simply want to advertise the product on their site and wait for people to buy it. Either way, this is free exposure and will allow you to gain an audience that would otherwise be inaccessible. Partaking in this type of venture also takes relatively little work on your part. All you have to do is reach out to a bunch of blogs and see if any of them are interested in working with you.

Activate the Powers of Social Media

Once you start selling product, it would be smart to set up social media accounts for your product as well. Once your accounts are up and running, you should also set a schedule for yourself to follow in regards to your posting frequency. Here is a list of the types of accounts you should consider setting up, along with a good schedule to follow:

Account Type	Posting Frequency
Twitter	At least 3 times per day, if not more
Facebook	No more than twice per day
Google+	No more than three times per day
LinkedIn	Once per day

If you think that you may not be able to keep track of a social media schedule on your own, there are plenty of free social media scheduling tools that exist on the web. A great one to consider is MassPlanner. This tool will allow you to consolidate your social media posting calendar in one easily accessible place. In order for this type of tactic to work for you, make sure that you're looking at the people who are liking and sharing your content. These are the types of people who are going to be most useful to you from a targeting perspective.

Don't let these people get away! Follow up with them in some manner.

Narrowing in On Your Target Audience

For any type of marketing, it's extremely important to understand that your audience is *not* everyone. This is an essential concept to understand, especially for the type of marketing that we're discussing. As a marketing professional, one of your jobs needs to be narrowing in on your target audience, rather than simply advertising to everyone and hoping that the people who are interested will find what you're selling. The reality is that advertisements are everywhere in our society. You don't want the product that you're selling to get lost in the shuffle. Below are a few questions that you should ask yourself that will help you to narrow in on who it is you should be looking for when you are attempting to sell your product:

1. **What problem does my product solve for people?** Present your product as a *solution* to this particular problem that your audience is facing.

2. **Who are your current customers?** Because of the fact that the company for whom you're working should already have a solid client base, you should be able to figure out the types of people who are gravitating towards the product that you're selling with relative ease. You should consider asking the company's sales team or people who have been working for the company for a while for this type of information.

3. **What are the Unique Features of the Product that You're Selling?** How does your product differ from the product of your competitor? These are the features that you should be emphasizing to your potential clients. Is there something that your product does that similar products don't? Tell your audience! These details

are sure to set your product apart from the rest.

This chapter has discussed ways that you can spend your time working towards network marketing success, both through physical means and digital means via the internet. Particularly with the online strategies that you can use for your sales practices, it's important to understand that neither of these approaches require that you develop a website of your own. Of course, you can certainly develop one if you wish to do so, but developing a website is often a time consuming and costly matter. This book seeks to offer strategies that are of the lowest possible cost to you, both from the perspective of your finances and time.

Chapter 4: Common Mistakes that New Network Marketers Make and How to Avoid Them

Now that you're fully aware of top tips to follow when network marketing and have also been given some concrete strategies that you can implement to find success, we will now turn our attention to the topic of mistakes that other network marketers commonly make. This may seem like a pessimistic topic to cover, but the reality is that if you are aware of these types of mistakes, there is less of a chance that you will make them yourself. With knowledge of these mistakes under your belt, you'll be in a much better position from an educational perspective, and this knowledge will be able to healthily influence your decisions in the future.

Common Mistake 1: Choosing to work for a company that focuses on recruiting more than it does sales generation

You need to make sure that you're choosing to work for a network marketing company that is focusing on the generation of new sales, rather than trying to primarily motivate you to recruit new people. If the company is not focusing the majority of its energy on selling the product, then how do you expect to ever make real money? This is a major problem that many newbie network marketers seem to miss. Don't allow yourself to be one of them!

Common Mistake 2: Targeting Friends and Family to No End

Obviously, when you're first starting out in the network marketing field, it can be tricky to find leads that are not members of your friends or family. Some coaching books and other forms of network marketing advice will tell you to make a list of 100 friends and family members who you can use as sources of lead generation when you're first starting, but this is not usually good advice. You want to push yourself to try to find legitimate leads, rather than pester your family and friends relentlessly. The harder that you work at finding true leads, the easier time you will have establishing real connections with people who are truly interested in your product over the long-term.

Common Mistake 3: Selling to your recruits, rather than attracting them

With network marketing, a key aspect of being successful is finding salespeople who are eager to work underneath of you; however, you need to be careful about how you attract these people. Many beginners will try and coerce people into becoming a seller underneath of them, instead of sitting back and attracting the people who are truly interested in this type of endeavor. When you sell to someone who is not truly a good fit for this type of work, you are setting both yourself and the person in question up for failure. You may find yourself making promises to this person that you will ultimately be unable to keep, and this person may also be someone who is going to only cause you headaches later on down the line. Be sure to find sellers who are going to work well with you, so that you can avoid unnecessary problems in the future.

Common Mistake 4: You fail to get out there and

sell

Even though this book discussed strategies that could be used on the internet, those tactics were not meant to replace the person-to-person tactics that you should be implementing from the jump. Remember, a key aspect of this type of marketing can be found in the name itself. If you do not network properly and constantly push yourself to attend as many events as you can, it is much less likely that you will end up seeing the sales numbers that you hope to anticipate.

Common Mistake 5: Talking negatively to the people working under you

It's important to remember that the people who are working under you should not be considered your friends. They are your employees, and their job is to make you a percentage of money every time that they make a sale. So often, people who are new to network marketing tend to consider their salespeople as friends. As the leader of this group, it's your job to constantly motivate your team to success. If instead of motivating, you're spending your time talking negatively about the company as a whole or about clients who are purchasing your product, you are setting a negative tone for the entire operation.

To rectify this type of problem, it is always a better idea to go to someone who is higher up on the chain than you are. Not only will this allow you to be perceived more positively by your sellers; it will also more likely lead to a sound solution to any problems that you may be having. Remember, you are in charge! It's important that you act like a leader. Otherwise, the negativity that you portray could begin to negatively influence the number of sales that you're generating, because your sales team feels discouraged and unsure. Be the approachable person you'd want your own boss to be, and you won't go wrong.

PART 2

INTRODUCTION

Spoken communication, even in the digital age, still stands as the most important way in which we interact with one another. Conversations trump other forms of communications such as texts and emails because unlike these less personal, digital forms, they offer the chance to make in-game adjustments in the present moment. When we exchange ideas and express our concerns in conversation it can be something of a chess match.

We want our 'moves' to ultimately create successful outcomes with the result of the conversation giving us what we hoped to accomplish. Before the conversation begins, we must give consideration to some important criteria – who it is we're talking to, what it is we want out of the conversation, and how will we prepare ourselves to have the conversation. We have to give some thought to these before considering the tactics we will employ as it is impractical to take a 'kitchen sink' approach to every conversation. The most effective conversation tactics are centered around wit, composure, politeness, consideration, flexibility, and guidance. These collectively help us to maintain quiet control over the conversation and enhance the probability that it will reach a positive conclusion. Conversations should build on one another and one way to gauge the direction of momentum is to have a brief follow-up for assurance that things are headed in the right direction.

CHAPTER 1: WHO ARE YOU TALKING TO?

For our purposes, a conversation is an exchange of verbally communicated ideas between two people. One of them is you, and the other is someone else. What is the degree of familiarity? Is it someone you've known all your life or is it that new co-worker that has been in the office for only a week? The relationship between those in the conversation helps establish a logical starting point.

An exchange between people who have only known each other professionally usually begins more formally than talk between two people who only know each other outside of their professional lives. It's appropriate to have 'small talk' precede the main focus in professional conversations due to the fact that people don't interact as often when this is the nature of the relationship and there are more uncertainties about one another.

With respect to personal relationships, there is a difference between what we shall call simple relationships and invested relationships. Because relationships have the potential to evolve, connections might be transitioning from simple to a more complex relationship such as that of a someone we've started to date or perhaps a new mother-in-law. In instances of changing connections, the capital and the stakes of conversations usually increase in value.

Certainly there are instances where two people are connected both personally and professionally, sometimes for a long period of time. Playing golf with business partners is a scenario that could lead to such a situation. This can be a little complicated, and one or both may tend to suspend the rules of engagement due to familiarity. This may require backing up and trying to have more formally constructed conversation.

If the person you're conversing with is someone new to you, it's really important to know yourself well and be aware of any personal tendencies or personality traits that might be perceived as 'a bit much' until others get to know you. Most of us can think of a personality quirk for just about anybody we know, including ourselves. Others who know us well have likely offered constructive criticism of the more challenging aspects of our personality and we should take this to heart.

CHAPTER 2: WHAT ARE YOUR MOTIVATIONS?

Any conversation has a purpose. Perhaps it is simply to maintain good relations in an established friendship. We engage in many conversations with no real purpose or objective in mind other than to maintain connection a light-hearted connection – as in the one we have perhaps with someone who we encounter once a week or so that works the check-out line in the grocery store.

Conversations don't always have a destination to be reached or some other tangible outcome, depending upon the nature of the relationship. Simple relationships such as with someone working the check-out line with who we might have a brief conversation in passing are quite different from more invested relationships, such as that with a romantic companion, relative, or professional colleague. Our motivations for engagement vary here and we need to have at least a small appreciation for the purpose, lest we lose track of what we might have invested.

Romantic and business conversations, different as they may be in terms of topics, tone, and other attributes of communication do have in common that we are talking about some level of investment on our part and presumably on the part of someone else as well. Whether it's someone we're thinking about proposing marriage or a merger, there's a lot of investment in either case.

All invested conversations require that the wants, needs, and demands of one person be measured alongside those of the other. Are you asking someone to help your business grow by offering an innovative analysis of sales data? Are you persuading your spouse that it's time for the family to grow with the addition of another child? An inventory will need to be taken in either scenario of the points that are shared in addition to where there are differences. Unless something goes terribly wrong and invested relationships dissolve, conversations will continue to occur and should reflect an effort on the part of two people to recall and maintain an awareness of what they are asking of each other.

CHAPTER 3: HOW WILL YOU PREPARE?

When a meeting is scheduled or a date is on the calendar, there is often much anticipation about how things will go. Anticipation leads to expectation or in some cases, reservation. Going over the possible outcomes in your mind followed up by a rehearsal or mock conversation is a good way to cover your bases and provide a sense of confidence about the impending conversation. If someone else is not available, read a dialogue with several exchanges as means to warm up before the actual conversation takes place

A number of variables can come into play that would affect preparation. A lot depends on whether the conversation taking place is between people in a new versus existing relationship. If the other person is new to you, other than being resourceful and gleaning some pertinent facts for conversation fodder, about all you can do is have some topics in mind in the event that the conversation stalls.

If you have the benefit of having past conversations with someone, this is helpful in that you can recall how that person tends to engage with you. Will they lead the conversation if you give them the chance or will they defer? In the cases where there is familiarity, more preparation will have to be put into a conversation that is anticipated to be strained. For instance, if conflict resolution is a likely aspect, think of appropriate questions ahead of time and ways to address issues that diffuse tension, and create a more relaxed environment. Think about acknowledging differences up front using a reconciliatory tone.

CHAPTER 4: WHICH TACTICS ARE INDISPENSABLE?

So we're at the point where introductions and small talk are over. From start to end, there are multiple tactics than can be employed to enhance the outcome, much like playing a hand of cards in a timely fashion.

Starting a conversation in amicable fashion is critical. Cut the small talk short or eliminate it if the other person is short on time or simply prefers to get down to business in short order. If it is your first conversation with someone, be mindful that you never get a second chance to make a first impression, and that impression, be it fair or not, may be formed very quickly. Early on acknowledge the other party's interests or concerns prior to stating your own, if you are the one to open things up or lead the conversation.

From start to finish, be constantly mindful and feel things out on everything from the tone of the conversation to how the other person is reacting. If a conversation gets out of hand or veers off course very far, it may be difficult to achieve the original goals that were set out. Quietly ask yourself "is everything going well, or should I try to make an adjustment?" If the other person stumbles or seems confused about how things are proceeding, try to improve clarity so that both of you are confident about how things are going relative to what might have been anticipated.

Being perceived as focused and giving the other person your full attention is perhaps the most important characteristic of someone who has productive conversations. If you come across as aloof or distracted it will probably be a downer. Someone may have taken a significant chunk of time out of their day to set aside for what they thought was going to be a meaningful exchange and instead they are totally deflated by someone who seems somewhere else.

We have already shed light on coming up with appropriate questions in advance for what are anticipated to be challenging conversations. This is particularly true if modern electronic communication or social media exchanges have preceded or led to the conversation. Incomplete thoughts or confusion created by these shorthand approaches to communicating may result in questions that should be dealt with at the beginning of the conversation. Heck, they may be the entire reason for the conversation. Giving prior thought to appropriate questions is good in any case as the most relevant questions may not come to mind if you wait until the conversation has begun. It is likely that the most curious questions, which reflect serious thought on your part, will come up in advance. Modify questions if you perhaps initially asked something too broad.

Maintain composure rather than get defensive when someone is confrontational or insulting. Disarming someone with a witty or playful response give you the control that they forfeited by deploying counterproductive language.

Give thorough responses that indicate you have respect for other peoples' questions. Abbreviated or literal responses in addition to being insufficiently clear, may also suggest a lack of respect or consideration for what the other person is trying to learn. If their facial expression or other observable response suggests that they did not get the information they were wanting, politely ask them to clarify what they were asking for if it is not abundantly clear.

Be mindful of where the conversation is going and be ready to get it back on track if it is headed into unproductive or counterproductive turf. Be prepared to usurp the role of leading the conversation should it stall. The other person might not be inclined to take the initiative here, and you may have no way of knowing if they're new to you.

Just like you shouldn't give a literal or abbreviated response, you shouldn't ask questions that would lead someone to think you were asking for such. Questions that demand responses beyond the mundane will give the other person a chance to share a more detailed account leaving them feeling as though they got to share the whole story.

People want to be recognized and given due credit. Do yourself a favor and take the opportunity in advance. If they feel the need to bring attention to an accomplishment before you mention it, they are indicating that they feel a lack of respect.

Recognition will make future conversations more productive because validation will motivate people to be more engaged.

We need to listen effectively in order to gain the respect of those we engage in conversation. Constantly cutting them off or interrupting them will make it seem as we are dismissing their importance in the relationship. One is not listening effectively if they are unable to stay in the present moment. Diverting the conversation may also be regarded as not respecting someone's concern about the topic at hand.

Making demands or requests in a conversation is a sensitive matter. Be fair and don't ask for too much. Don't ask for something if it is going to be obvious that you haven't done anything to help yourself and just want to place a burden on the other person. No one wants to feel as though they're being taken advantage of, so consider carefully as to whether you should make a request of them.

Demonstrate that you are in the moment by actions that are visibly obvious. Record notes during the conversation or commitments you have made. Place a future date on your phone calendar when an event is mentioned. This implies intent on your part to follow through and makes the other person feel as though they've gotten something across to you and that their input was worthwhile.

CHAPTER 5: THE SUPREME TACTIC – THE FOLLOW-UP CONVERSATION

After a conversation, you must take inventory of how things went. If you know of strategic mistakes that were made along the way, make note of them and take care not to commit them in future conversations. You must hold yourself responsible for being able to recall any specific outcomes and good note-taking is the best way to accomplish this.

If a conversation ends with both parties knowing what was specifically agreed to or are certain of specific commitments that were made and how outcomes are to be achieved, it may not be necessary to revisit the conversation down the road. When outcomes aren't certain and nothing was specifically agreed upon, it may be in the best interest of two people to come back together and express their views about what each took from the conversation. Revisit the points of agreement and disagreement with emphasis given as to why sentiments differed on particular subjects that were discussed. An apologetic tone might be called for if you lost your composure or you felt deficient in attention or focus. Remember that follow-up conversation may be used as a polite gesture to offer thanks or appreciation, in which case they needn't be extended affairs. If a follow-up is something of an in-between linking two major conversations, it may require more input as it establishes what will be discussed in the latter conversation.

PART 3

Chapter one: Prospecting - What is it?

What prospecting is was briefly touched on in the introduction. When you are prospecting, you are working towards the end goal of getting potential prospects into a sale so that they become a customer that generates revenue for you.

There are some people that do not understand what the difference is between a lead and a prospect. A lead is going to be someone who is a potential customer that has to show some sort of interest in your company or the services that you offer. This can be someone who has visited your website, subscribed to your newsletter, or anything that has gotten them looking into your company.

A prospect is going to be someone who is not a lead but is most likely going to become a customer. These are the people that you target to get them interested in your company. These are the people who have not had any interaction with your company, and if they have, then they have had limited interaction.

Ultimately, your goal is going to be the same as a lead or a prospect; you are going to want to get them to be a customer for your company.

Here is the funnel that you are going to follow to try and get a potential customer to be an actual customer.

Step one: do your research and see if you should follow the lead or let it go. You most likely have a set of criteria that you are going to go through to see how likely it is that the lead or prospect that you are looking at is going to become a customer and if you should pursue them or if you should move on to the next one. The customer relationship management software is going to be the software that you are going to use to track customers and potential customers so that you can see where they are in the sales process.

Step two: after you have determined if the lead is one that will hopefully pan out, you are going to need to connect to your target through prospecting. Someone who is in charge of contacting these leads is going to be the person that is going to reach out to them and talk to them. But, before you can reach out to them, you need to take this prospect to the person that is going to make the ultimate decision on if you should reach out to them or not. This person is typically going to be your boss, and you are most likely going to have to go through their receptionist to talk to them.

Step three: after the "decision maker" has said that it is alright, you will then either pass the information on to the next person, or you will connect to the prospect. This is going to be the initial call that you are going to make to reach out to this person and try and push them towards being a customer.

Step four: in the first call with your prospect, you

are going to learn about your customer and learn what their needs are. If you think that your company can meet the needs of your prospect, then you are going to be able to move them along in the sales process. There are some things that you are going to have to fight against when it comes to getting your prospect further in the sales process. That is going to be things the prospect is going to worry about such as their budget, how long it is going to take to get the product you are offering, so on and so forth.

Step five: close your sale! Not every prospect is going to become a customer. But, when you close a won sale, you are going to have turned a prospect into a customer. However, when you have a close-lost that means that you did not get a new customer. Hopefully, your closed-won outweigh your closed-lost.

Chapter TWO:

Techniques to Use for Prospecting

There are two main types of prospecting that you are going to do, outbound and inbound.

Outbound prospecting:

Cold calling: this will be calls that are unsolicited as you attempt to sell your product or service.

Social spamming: messages that are sent on social media that are unsolicited to sell the product or service.

When you do outbound prospecting, you are typically not going to have any contact history with the client. You are essentially trying to reach out to the person and create some connection with them that is going to put your company in their head, so when they begin to look for the product or service that you have to offer, they are going to think of you first.

Inbound Prospecting:

Warm emailing: you are going to be reaching out to someone who has expressed some kind of interest in your company before, and you want to see if there can possibly be a relationship with that person.

Social selling: social media can be used to explore relationships as well. With social media, a sales representative has the ability to answer any questions that a lead may have about the products and services that they see your company has to offer. If they cannot give the answer right there, then they can send that person in the right direction to get the answer that they are looking for.

Doing research for inbound prospecting is not going to be as extensive because the person has already interacted with your company in some way. All you are going to be doing is reaching out to that person to try and get them to spend money with your company.

It is suggested that you try and stick to inbound prospecting because most people are going to decide on if they are going to purchase a product when they hear about the product from someone that they trust. This can be from a friend of a family member, and it can be face to face or on social media.

There is a smaller amount of people who buy products because of media reports or other analyst reports.

What a lot of sales people do not realize is that whenever they "start" their sales process, they are already most of the way through it because there are not many prospects that do not have some kind of knowledge about what you are trying to sell.

In order to be successful, realize that the buyer most likely has the knowledge that you are wanting them to have. Therefore, you need to modify how you reach out to these potential buyers and rather than treat them like they do not know anything about you, educate yourself on what they do know and fill in any blanks that may be missing in the information that they already possess.

Chapter three: How to be Successful in Your Prospecting

Every company is going to have their own processes when it comes to prospecting. However, you are not going to want to become part of the sales statistic where around fifty percent of your prospecting is not productive. You are going to pick the approach that is going to work best for you and go from there. But, while you are doing that, you will have a few steps that you need to follow to be successful.

Step one: Target

You need to know who you need to talk to in order to get the sale. Too many times the contact person is going to try and start at the bottom of the company's totem pole and work their way up. This is when they tend to get stopped because you cannot get to the person that you actually need to talk to. So, before you can start contacting your prospects, you need to make sure that you have the appropriate people on that list. Your list needs to be clean and ready to go before you begin reaching out.

Step two: Value

You may have a script that you have to follow when you are talking to your prospect. But you do not have to follow it word for word. Put a personal touch to who you are speaking to. If you make a customer feel valued, then they are most likely going to spend more money with your company than if you just treat them like your company does not value them and they are just another number in your books. When you treat someone like they matter, then they are not only going to let your boss know how good you did with the sale, but they are going to request to speak to you personally when they are ready to order more product.

Step three: The right offer

Your company probably has some sort of offer that you can offer your customers. Before a customer closes a deal, they are going to want to know that they are getting the highest quality product at a reasonable price. But, interim offers that are made need to be created with care because you do not want to create an offer that causes you to lose money just for that customer.

Step four: No tricks

There is no need to cut corners when you are talking to customers. Think of it like this, if you would not tell your boss something, then do not say anything when it comes to your prospecting. Not everything has to be disclosed right up front, but you do need to be honest with your customer so that they do not feel like they are being ripped off by your company.

Step Five: Multiple touches

Often times it takes multiple tries to get ahold of someone because they are going to be busy. This usually means that many companies are having up to ten different people touch the same record before you finally get ahold of who it is that you are wanting to talk to.

Step six: Variety

Do not just stick to phone calls to your prospects. Send them mail and emails as well. While you are going to be trying to reach out to the prospect in several different ways, you need to remember to put some value in it! Look back at step two!

By following these six steps, you are going to have a higher chance of being successful when it comes to your prospecting than someone who does not.

Chapter four: Prospecting Myths

No one wants to be rejected when they are trying to make their sales. However, much like anything else, there are going to be myths that are going to surround prospecting to cause people to stray away from prospecting. Within this section of this book, you are going to learn some of the myths that surround small business prospecting.

1. Prospecting is just used for sales.

No! Prospecting is not used for sales at all. While you are prospecting, you may find someone who wants to buy from you, but that is not your goal. With prospecting, you are going to be trying to sort through the list of those that you have to reach out to and getting rid of the ones that are not interested in buying from your company. Those that are interested are going to cause the sales process to begin, but not everyone is going to want to go through this process.

2. Prospecting is nothing but a numbers game.

Many people associate prospecting with cold calls, and while cold calls are one of the prospecting techniques, you are wanting to put quality into your prospecting rather than quantity. As we discussed earlier in the book, if you make a customer feel valued, then they are most likely going to take that sales process to the next step.

3. Scripts are for kids

Scripts offer some sort of framework for how you are going to try and pull in someone when you are talking to them. You are going to have the answers to questions that they are going to be asking you. However, if you are allowed to, you can deviate from the script so that you can provide a more personalized experience for the client.

4. Prospecting is going to take time

It is not going to take you long before you know if you are going to have someone who wants to go on to the next step in the sales process or not. Not only that, but they are going to let you know if they are able to afford what it is that you are selling or not. Armed with that knowledge, you are going to be able to know when to move on and when you can keep going.

5. Close them on the appointment

Many prospects are going to agree to meet with your company because they do not want to tell you no over the phone and it is just easy to agree to meet in person than telling you no. Instead of doing this, if you think that a prospect may be interested, try a different approach such as sending them an information pack that is going to tell them more about your company and what you have to offer. If they want to move on to the next step, let them come to you!

Chapter Five: Tools to Use for Prospecting

Tools for prospecting are going to make it to where you are able to manage relationships better with your prospects, and you are able to maximize your productivity. It will also assist in making sure that you do not lose track of where you are in your process with that particular customer.

Tools for your prospect list

Are you buying your list or are you creating one? Depending on your answer to that question, will depend on what tool you are going to use. When you purchase a prospect list, you are going to be taking on a lot of risk because the list is not always going to be reliable. Therefore, buying the list should be your last resort. In order to build your prospect list, you can use one of these tools.

1. Salesloft prospector: this tool is used with Google Chrome and is going to get the contact information from social media networks.
2. Broadlook capture: you are going to be able to get the information that you need about a prospect from any document or website that has any mention of them. With this information, you are going to possibly get a lot of information that is going to educate you properly on the prospect that you are looking at.
3. Data.com: this database is going to look through over a million different listings for possible prospects for you.
4. Sidekick for business: this database is going to give you around sixteen million business that you are going to be able to sort through to find

the perfect prospects for you based on what it is that you are looking for.

Managing emails

When you are using email marketing, it is going to be dependent on time. If you send out too many messages then you are going to find that you are not being found in someone's inbox due to the fact that you are pushed to the spam folder, but if you do not send out enough, you are going to be overlooked and not have any lasting impact on your prospect.

1. Sidekick for business: once again, Sidekick is going to enable you to schedule emails to send out to your prospects and get notifications whenever your website is visited by a prospect.
2. Outreach.io: the outreach tool only does one thing, but it is very good at it. With outreach, you are going to be able to set up touchpoints

for our prospects so that you can detect replies from your prospects and offers you tools where you can see when a message is converted and why it was converted.

3. Salesloft cadence: whenever you set your sales up front, you can use salesloft to set up email templates as well as reminders so that you can send out the emails whenever they need to be sent out. At the point in time that a prospect sends you an email, then that prospect will be removed from the cadence program.

4. Salesforce.com enterprise workflows: in using this tool you are going to create automatic workflows. The biggest downside to this is that it does not have many of the advanced features that other tools have to offer you.

Sales calls

Emails are not going to get all of your work done. You are going to have to call them as well, especially those that turn out to be cold leads. Most of the time it is only going to take one phone call to set up a relationship or to close a deal. But, when you combine the call with emails, you are going to be able to close even more deals because you are going to be able to get out all of the information that the client is going to need to make their decision.

1. Close.io: this program is a CRM program that is fully integrated. This is going to be the program that you use when all other programs do not fulfill what it is that you are looking for. Close.io is an all in one CRM program.
2. Ringio: with Ringio, you are going to receive a sales telephony platform that is integrated. This program is going to work with other programs such as Salesforce and Zoho so that all of our data is synced and calls are recorded

in order to use them for training in making your productivity better.

Chapter Six: Tips for Prospecting

These tips are going to help you in your prospecting so that if you are doing calls, you are able to crush your next call and possibly even close the deal! And, if you are new to prospecting, these tips are going to help make it to where you are one step ahead of the game.

1. Confidence! Do not let your voice waver whenever you are talking to a customer. Even if you do not know the answer to the question that they ask, do not let them know that. Simply inform them that you are going to find that answer for them. Keep in mind that they do not know who you are and they cannot see you. Besides, having confidence is going to be the number one way that you are going to close a deal.

2. Mistakes are going to happen. You are human, and you are going to make mistakes. Do not beat yourself up over this. Just move on and learn from your mistakes. There are going to be calls that are going to end up being bad, and there are going to be calls that are going to go perfectly. Do not let the bad ones keep you from moving on.

3. Know when a prospect is not a good fit. Do not continue to try and push products on a prospect that is not showing any interest in what it is that you are trying to sell. Also, if the client flat out says that they are not interested in what it is that you are promoting, thank them and move on. You do not want to keep going with a prospect when it is nothing but a dead end.

4. Be a consultant. While you are trying to sell a product, you do not have to push it on them.

Educate them instead. The sale will come later.

5. Leverage is going to improve your sales. Try and make sure that you are well aware of the marketing process of your company so that you can know what each buyer is going through when it comes to what they are looking for to meet their needs. Once you know what it is that your customer is looking for, you are going to have a better idea of what to offer them.

6. Do not be afraid to ask questions. You need to understand as much about your customer as you possibly can so that you can make sure that you are meeting their needs or moving on because they are not a good fit with your company.

7. Do not give up at the first sign of objection. You are going to come across prospects that

are going to give you excuses such as their budget. Many times these objects to see what you are going to offer them or because they want more information from you. Do not stop just because they throw up a yellow flag, offer them some more information and see if you can break through that objection.

8. Be energetic. While prospecting is going to be a tiring job, you should not let your prospect know that you are tired. Keep your energy up so that your prospect does not know what is truly going on behind the scenes. If you voice lacks enthusiasm, they are going to wonder why they should pick your company over someone else's.

Conclusion

Thank you for making it through to the end of *Recruiting & Retailing Mastery for Network Marketing: How You Can Become the Next Network Marketing Superstar in Your Company.*

The next step is to start looking for a reputable network marketing company for whom you can work, if you have not already done so. Once you've found a company about which you're excited, the next step is to think about how you can best captivate your audience via the internet and a strong personal presence. Next, create your schedule for success that we discussed in chapter 3 of this book, and start selling! As you go through the process of becoming more successful through the network marketing tactics that were presented in this book, be sure to always keep in mind the last chapter that was on the topic of common mistakes to avoid. With all of this information in your head, there's no doubt that you're going to increase your sales over the long-term. Lastly, remember that you can always use this book as a reference guide whenever you feel like you need some quick guidance. That's what it's here for!

THANK YOU

Dear treasured reader, I would like to thank you from the bottom of my heart for choosing to purchase this book. I hope you've gotten some valuable information that you can use right now to build a successful online business for yourself.

In case you missed it earlier, if you would like to receive latest tips and tricks on internet marketing, exclusive strategies, upcoming books & promotions, and **more,** do subscribe to my mailing list in the link below! I will be giving away a free book that you can download *right away* as well after you subscribe to show my appreciation!

Once again thank you and all the best to your success!
Jonathan S. Walker

About The Author

Hi there it's Jonathan Walker here, I want to share a little bit about myself so that we can get to know each other on a deeper level. I grew up in California, USA, and have lived there for the better part of my life. Being exposed to many different people and opportunities when I was young, it made me want to strive to become an entrepreneur to escape the rat race path that most of my peers had taken. I knew I wanted to be able to travel and experience the world the way it was meant to be seen and I've done just that. I've travelled to most places around the world and I'm enjoying every minute of it for sure. In my free time I love to play tennis and believe it or not, compose songs. I wish you all the best again in your endeavours, and may your dreams, whatever they may be, come true abundantly in the near future.

www.ingramcontent.com/pod-product-compliance
Lightning Source LLC
LaVergne TN
LVHW010408070526
838199LV00065B/5915